The New

Survival Guide

by **Sabrina Holcomb**

with **Ed Amundson** and **Patti Ralabate**

NEA Professional Library

Library of Congress Cataloging-in-Publication Data

The new IDEA survival guide.
   p. cm.
   "An NEA Professional Library publication."
   Includes bibliographical references.
   ISBN 0-8106-2016-2
   1. Handicapped children—Education—United States—Handbooks, manuals, etc.
   2. Individualized education programs—United States—Handbooks, manuals, etc.
   I. NEA Professional Library (Association)

   LC4031 .N49 2000
   371.9'04394—dc21

                                                          00-050115

      LC4031 .H622000

      Holcomb, Sabrina.

      The new IDEA survival
        guide /

TABLE OF CONTENTS

ACKNOWLEDGMENTS

Our appreciation is extended to the following people for their invaluable contributions and for helping us put *The New IDEA Survival Guide* into the hands of the educators who make a quality education possible for all students.

We would particularly like to acknowledge Sam Pizzigati for the vision and guidance that made this project possible; Faye Northcutt, Mellisa Williams, and Nesa Chappelle for the information and resources provided by NEA's Teaching and Learning division; Diane Shust, Leslie Collins, and Michael Simpson for their legal advice; Troy Justesen and JoLeta Reynolds for their professional guidance; Bronna Zlochiver for her editorial assistance; Ann Marie Bohan for her production expertise; and Vanessa Nugent and Hallie Shell for their inspired design work.

We would also like to thank the following members of the NEA IDEA/ Special Education Resource Cadre for supplying some of the "voices" of the educators in this book: Judith Basa, Ron Benner, Mary Binegar, Charlene L. Christopher, Carol Comparsi, Ellen Dunn, Cheryl Ervin, Rosemary King Johnston, M. Elaine Kresge, Walker McGinnis, Julie Moore, Charles Nelson, Bernadette Ortega, Judith Richards, Noel Richardson, Sharon Schultz, Katherine Starrett, Barbara Taub-Albert, Sarah Thomas, and Carol Walsh.

INTRODUCTION

The National Education Association has a long and proven history of advocating for appropriate educational opportunities for all students, and NEA has strongly supported educating students with disabilities within the nation's public schools since the 1975 passage of the original federal special education law (PL 94-142). Nonetheless, meeting the challenge of educating students with disabilities alongside their nondisabled peers has never been easy.

In the mid-1990s, after nearly twenty-five years of "mainstreaming" and "inclusion," a complex political and emotional atmosphere surrounded congressional attempts to reauthorize the federal special education law, now known as the Individuals with Disabilities Education Act (IDEA). Many believed that IDEA was a good law that needed strengthening, some thought the legislation should be left alone, and others thought it should be eliminated completely. Within this atmosphere, Congress began designing the new law. As both the Senate and the House drafted their versions, it quickly became apparent that this would be a highly contentious effort.

At this critical point in the process, NEA helped bring together a diverse group to develop a unified proposal. Among the groups represented were the American Federation of Teachers, the American Association of School Administrators, the Association of Retarded Citizens, the Consortium of Citizens with Disabilities, the Council of Great City Schools, the National Association of Elementary School Principals, the National Association of Secondary School Principals, the National Parents Network on Disabilities, the National School Boards Association, and other interested parties. Over several days of discussion, this unique coalition was able to develop a set of principles that became the framework for the final version of the law.

The final document was a testament to compromise. As in any compromise, however, no one group got everything it wanted. While some of the changes were not as extensive as NEA members may have hoped, they did represent major movement in key areas that included:

- Student discipline
- Professional development
- Role of general education teachers
- Health services
- Paperwork reduction

- Litigation costs
- Federal funding
- Graduation standards

The Individuals with Disabilities Education Act of 1997 became the first major reauthorization of IDEA since 1975. Since its passage, it has served as a base for minimum requirements, but some states and local districts have added extra requirements to the new law's provisions. Some states have revised their state statues to comply with the federal law; some have not.

This book aims to help NEA members who are charged with implementing the provisions of IDEA '97 by:

- clarifying what the federal law actually says. (NEA members should check with their state officials to determine whether their state laws or regulations provide greater protection to students with disabilities.)
- correcting myths and misinformation about what IDEA '97 does and does not mandate.
- informing NEA members about how to be active participants in developing their students' programs.
- recommending how NEA members may creatively address specific difficulties they may encounter.
- suggesting how school teams can develop innovative programs to meet student needs.
- leading NEA members to additional resources.

We believe that IDEA '97 can be a catalyst to help NEA members advocate for their students, themselves, and their colleagues. We hope the information in this book will help all of us provide appropriate educational opportunities to all of our students.

Ed Amundson
Chair, NEA Caucus for Educators of Exceptional Children
NEA Cross-Unit Work Team on IDEA and Special Education

Patti Ralabate
NEA Caucus for Educators of Exceptional Children
NEA Cross-Unit Work Team on IDEA and Special Education

A Good IDEA?

As America enters a new century, it's hard to imagine that an entire class of citizens is still struggling with discrimination and segregation. Not too long ago these citizens were denied equal access to employment, public facilities, and educational opportunities. In fact, federal legislation was required to rectify this inequality.

It wasn't the Civil Rights Act of 1964 or Brown v. Board of Education of 1954, but the Vocational and Rehabilitation Act of 1973 that banned discrimination against individuals with disabilities by any federally funded program or activity. Later, it took a series of class action suits brought by parent advocates to compel the passage of PL 94-142, the original federal special education law.

All children with disabilities in this country were guaranteed the right to a free and appropriate public education (FAPE) only a little more than 25 years ago. This achievement may not have captured the nation's attention like the first day African-American students walked into the public schools of Little Rock. Nevertheless, the first day students with disabilities wheeled off a yellow bus into a neighborhood school, a new entitlement to public education and a new civil rights movement had begun. The comparisons between the struggles to end racial discrimination and discrimination against students with disabilities do not end here.

As racial desegregation and integration progressed across America, some teachers' voices were raised in protest and concern. Some felt inadequately prepared to meet the diverse needs of these new students in their classrooms. Their own experiences afforded little, if any, contact with the culture of the students they were to teach. States, local districts, and colleges helped by offering workshops and classes on multicultural diversity. In the meantime, a generation of future teachers grew up in a new culture where they sat in school side-by-side with students of racial backgrounds different from their own.

In the late 1970s, the advent of federal special education law PL 94-142 confronted many teachers with similar challenges. Few teachers had had contact with disabled students during their schooling because most students with disabilities were relegated to segregated state institutions or schools. A new generation of teachers raised concerns about their lack of knowledge and experience teaching students with special needs, and, in response, states, local districts, and colleges provided awareness workshops and classes.

A Shift in Emphasis

Nonetheless, we can only take the similarities between the two civil rights experiences so far. Special education, as originally defined in PL 94-142, carried its own source of funding and specially trained teachers. As it was implemented across the country, special education evolved into a separate place or adjunct program "mainstreamed" into what was known as the "general education environment." Special education teachers, and the students they taught, usually functioned outside of general education. While planning student programs, educators had to actually justify the reasons why students with disabilities would be receiving their education or services within the general education environment.

By the late-1990s, when Congress revisited how educational programs would be provided to students with disabilities, there had been a 180-degree shift in emphasis. Research was showing that, for the most part, students with disabilities performed better in general education classrooms, and lawmakers wanted these students to be given appropriate access to the general education curriculum. Many lawmakers were thinking in terms of physical disabilities, however, and, at the time, few realized the impact students with behavioral difficulties, severe learning disabilities, and medical disabilities would have on the general education environment.

Under the reauthorized federal special education law, now known as the Individuals with Disabilities Education Act of 1997 (IDEA '97), we must first consider providing services to students with disabilities within the general education environment. In planning a student's program, educators must now justify reasons why a given student is *not* being taught within the general education classroom. For many, this new approach represents a major shift in core beliefs.

The main principle of IDEA '97: Students with disabilities should be educated within the general education classroom with appropriate aids and services, if necessary—a viewpoint that flies in the face of the traditional "pull-out" special education programs and self-contained classes that have evolved, in some districts, into isolated programs with their own curriculum, materials, and staff.

Enhancing Best Practices

Under IDEA '97, school districts must still make a full continuum of service and placement options available. But an underlying belief of the new law assumes that most students with disabilities can be taught the same curriculum successfully and held to the same standards as their nondisabled peers. Several new elements under IDEA '97 reflect current research and best practices and hold the potential for significantly changing how students with disabilities are educated within the public schools. Some of the most promising are:

Classroom-based assessments. Classroom-based assessments can be included during the student's referral and identification process. This will require active participation of the general education classroom teacher and will provide student data that is instructionally relevant.

Determining eligibility. When deciding whether a student is eligible for special education and related services, certain conditions must be considered. A student may not be eligible for services if it's determined that the primary reason for his or her lack of progress is due to limited English proficiency or a lack of instruction in reading or math. This enhances the importance of the work of general education school-based teams, such as child study teams or early intervention programs for at-risk students.

Classroom-oriented goals. A discussion of the student's strengths, as well as the ways in which the child's disability affects his or her involvement and progress in the general curriculum, should lead to positive, classroom-oriented goals.

Accessing general education curriculum. All students with disabilities must have access to the general education curriculum and, as appropriate, be held to the same standards as other students who are not disabled. Student goals and objectives should be classroom-focused. This increases the opportunity for school staff to collaborate in goal setting and instruction. The design of the reauthorized IDEA helps eliminate the barriers that may have prevented innovative teaching strategies at the school site level in the past.

Incidental benefits. Under a provision called "permissive use of funds," it's now allowable for one or more nondisabled students to benefit from the services and aids provided to a student with a disability in a general classroom setting. This little-known provision of the law, referred to by some educators as incidental benefits, offers the prospect of enhancing learning for all students.

Accommodations and modifications. Most practitioners are currently using strategies and methods that make accommodations for the diverse learners in their classes. Learning how to use various accommodations and modifications for students with disabilities should increase the teaching "bag-of-tricks" for all classroom teachers and paraeducators. This can enhance learning opportunities for all students.

Teamwork. Ideally, the team process used to develop an Individualized Education Program (IEP) could benefit all students. In order for a team to function well, its members learn from and share with each other. A good team has well-established open channels of communication and consults regularly in a dynamic manner. Team decisions are made by consensus and recognize the needs of the student, family, and staff members. The team also has ample administrative supports, including opportunities for professional development and time to collaborate. And, most important, the team has a set of common goals.

The Challenge Ahead

IDEA '97, while not technically a civil rights statute, is sometimes referred to as both a civil rights law and an education law because it has created enforceable rights to a free and appropriate public education for students with disabilities. The new version of the law will substantially change how we teach students with disabilities, as well as their nondisabled peers.

As with any major change, both exciting possibilities and frustrations lie ahead. Significant shifts in beliefs and expectations will result. And, as with any change, adapting will take time. For most of us, the challenge ahead is not just to survive IDEA '97 but to take full advantage of its opportunities.

The following chapters are organized around questions that real teachers across the country are asking. The question-and-answer format leads you through a number of scenarios that address educators' most pressing concerns about the new IDEA, while identifying strategies and resources to help you address five critical areas:

1. developing the Individualized Education Program (IEP)
2. managing paperwork
3. handling discipline issues
4. getting appropriate professional development
5. communicating with parents

2

Developing IEPs

"How can I possibly meet the curriculum standards for this student? I'm especially worried that this child will take all of my attention and that I won't have time for the rest of my students."

Scene 1—What Is My Role as a General Education Teacher?

Stephanie, a student with a severe learning disability, is entering my classroom this year. I've just been informed that I'm going to be a member of Stephanie's IEP team. This is new territory for me. What is my role?

Each student who receives special education and related services under IDEA must have an Individualized Education Program, or IEP. And one of the most significant changes in the new IDEA is the inclusion of at least one of the student's general education teachers on the IEP team. As a content specialist, it's critical for you to be involved in the process of developing Stephanie's IEP. You're the educator with the knowledge base to develop an appropriate IEP as it relates to the curriculum. You'll also be able to suggest supplementary aids, services, or changes to the IEP that will help you do your job and help Stephanie reach her full potential.

Who are the other members of the IEP team?

The IEP team should include the following people:

- parent and/or legal guardian
- special education teacher
- general education teacher
- individual who can interpret instructional implications of evaluation results

- other individuals—at the discretion of the parent or agency—who have special knowledge or expertise about the student, including related services personnel
- school system representative who is qualified to provide or supervise specially designed instruction for children with disabilities and who is knowledgeable about the general curriculum and the availability of resources
- transition services agency representative, for students at least 14 and over
- student, as appropriate

Will I get any release time for IEP meetings? Where and how often will they take place?

The IEP team usually meets at the school site at least once a year, although additional meetings may be necessary. As the general education teacher, you may not have to be present throughout an entire IEP meeting, or participate in discussions about issues for which you have no responsibility. The IEP team helps decide how much of your participation is needed, depending on the nature of the student's needs and the purpose of the IEP meeting.

IEP meetings can be held at varying times. If necessary, you can ask your principal for release time to attend these meetings. Some best practices include writing release time into the IEP for future meetings, holding IEP meetings during a common planning period, providing substitutes for classroom teachers if the meetings are held during the school day, and providing remuneration if the meetings are held after school hours. Some school districts have contract language that promotes these practices.

Whether or not you physically attend the IEP meeting, the school district is required to provide you with access to the student's IEP. In addition, you must be informed of your responsibilities in implementing the IEP. For example, if certain accommodations or modifications need to be in place in your classroom, you should be notified.

When will I get time to meet with members of the IEP team outside of IEP meetings?

During the course of the school year, you may need to meet with the special education teacher or other members of Stephanie's team to share information and implement the program. Team members need time to confer on an ongoing basis and the support of the administration to provide for that time.

Enlightened administrators are employing a number of different strategies to provide adequate planning time for their staff:

Joint planning time. Several classes of students are scheduled to attend art, music, or special lessons while their general and special education teachers meet.

Grade-level meetings. Special education teachers attend grade-level staff meetings to confer with general education teachers.

Weekly conference times. Some districts have built weekly conference times into their teachers' schedules. Also, individual teachers frequently establish informal meeting times to confer.

Whatever strategies you use, it helps to have supportive administrators who realize that planning time is crucial.

How do I make sure I get the information and support I need to teach Stephanie?

Supports for personnel can be written into an IEP and can take a number of different forms:

Staff training. The team can write into the IEP that all staff working with the student will receive appropriate training, at no extra cost to the staff. For instance, if a student has autism, staff members may need training in how to deal with that specific disability.

Classroom aides. Some IEPs may require paraeducators as classroom aides. Paraeducators who are properly trained and supervised can work with individual students, small groups, or the entire class. These aides may provide necessary physical, as well as academic, support.

Co-teaching. In many schools, general education and special education teachers are co-teaching classes. IDEA '97 allows for increased flexibility in addressing the needs of all students. One result is that special education personnel can now teach within the general education environment, even if the students they are working with are not identified as having special needs. This can reduce the burden on both teachers and provide a wonderful opportunity for all of the students to benefit from the expertise and attention of two professionals.

Release time. Conference time for IEP meetings can be included in the IEP under support for personnel.

Supports for the student, in the form of accommodations and modifications, can be written into the IEP as well. Accommodations usually involve changes made to materials, facilities, or work time. Modifications usually involve changes in workload or curriculum expectations.

Am I supposed to make sure Stephanie keeps up with my general education students?

Yes, if that's the stated goal in the IEP. Your expectations for Stephanie's performance level will depend on what's in her IEP. Your general curriculum will not change. Instead, you'll work in conjunction with Stephanie's special education teacher to develop accommodations and modifications that will allow Stephanie to learn material from the general curriculum. For example, if

Stephanie has fine-motor difficulties due to her disability, she might be allowed to do part of the math homework, or she might need an assistive technology device, such as a laptop, to help her complete all of the math problems. If her disability involves memory difficulties, she might be allowed to use an open book during an exam or listen to a book on tape. There are many examples of assistive technology devices—such as laptops, books on tape, and voice recognition software—that can help Stephanie and other students with disabilities access the general curriculum.

But is it really fair for Stephanie to receive this special treatment, then be graded the same as the other students?

In such cases, the definition of fair does not mean equal treatment. Fair means that each student receives what he or she needs to be successful and reach his or her full potential. Teachers make reasonable accommodations for other students on a daily basis.

For example, eyeglasses are an accommodation. If a student breaks or forgets his or her glasses, the teacher would move the student closer to the board or have another student read to the student who needs glasses. This is not considered an unfair advantage, but something the student needs in order to be successful.

If a student in your math class has just arrived in this country and does not yet speak or read English well enough to tackle math word problems, you might allow the student to skip the word problems and just do the calculations. Or you could have someone translate the word problems into the student's native language. You've modified the work the student is doing but still provided an opportunity for him or her to learn the material.

Do Stephanie's other general education teachers have a right to attend her IEP meeting if they have not been asked to do so? How can only one general education teacher speak for the other content specialists?

You have the right to ask to attend a meeting and the right to go, if invited by the parents or school administrators. If you have not been asked to participate, however, the actual logistics are a gray area. You may want to consider the following suggestions:

- Suppose a high-school student has five general education teachers, and they all want to attend the meeting. Since, in some cases, general education teachers are not required to sit in on the entire meeting, they may be able to rotate through the meeting, replacing each other as soon as they've finished discussing their subject area.

- If the team's general education teacher has already been designated, you can ask to attend as the "individual who has special knowledge or expertise about the student." As one of Stephanie's teachers, you fit that description.

- Stephanie's parents can invite you to be a member of the IEP team if you have special knowledge or expertise about their child. Parents can be your best advocates. Developing a good working relationship with them can be an advantage to both you and your student.

- Some secondary schools are passing out forms to all of a student's teachers before the IEP meeting. The filled-in forms are then shared at the meeting.

- As one of Stephanie's teachers, you can request that an IEP meeting be scheduled in order to discuss possible changes in her program. If the administration chooses not to schedule a meeting, and your continued efforts to resolve some of your concerns are not successful, you can contact your local or state NEA affiliate to request assistance.

What if I disagree with the other members of Stephanie's team on her placement or some other aspect of her program? Who makes the final decision?

IEP teams do not take a formal vote, but final decisions are usually the result of a majority opinion. Once a decision is made, an administrator cannot legally negate the team's decision; however, if parents disagree they may follow due process procedures or opt for mediation. If a teacher doesn't agree with the team, he or she can write a dissenting opinion, which should be attached to the student's IEP form and become a part of the record. Some districts have a place on the IEP form for dissenting opinions. This document will be helpful later on if the teacher needs to call another meeting and ask for changes or additions to the student's IEP.

How do I protect myself from retaliation if I'm in disagreement with the administration or district over a student's IEP or my role in the process?

Are your concerns in your student's best interests? Individuals who are advocating on behalf of the disabled are protected from retaliation under Section 504 of the Rehabilitation Act of 1973, as amended, and Title II of the Americans with Disabilities Act. Document all of your efforts, and if you do have any problems, your local affiliate will be in a better position to help you.

Scene 2—What Is My Role as a Special Education Teacher?

I'm a special education teacher, and I've been told that the new IDEA requires me to write IEP goals and objectives based on the state curriculum standards and the general curriculum. This is not my area of expertise. Do I really need to become a curriculum specialist to develop goals and objectives for my students?

No, you'll work with other members of the team to develop an IEP that meets curriculum standards. As a special education teacher, you bring your expertise on instructional strategies to the team, while the general education teacher brings his or her expertise on standards-based information. Also, academic standards are not the only expectations used to write a student's goals and objectives; behavioral expectations may be written into the IEP as well.

As the special education teacher, you're no longer expected to be the pull-out expert who takes students with special needs and "fixes" them in seclusion. IDEA '97 provides special education teachers with an opportunity to work in collaboration with their colleagues as opposed to working in isolation. As a result of this collaboration, special education teachers are becoming more knowledgeable about the general curriculum, and general education teachers are, in turn, learning more about appropriate instructional strategies.

How can the general education teacher and I work together to develop goals and objectives that meet or address curriculum standards?

While general education teachers are content specialists, special education teachers are well versed in instructional strategies and the types of modifications their students need in order to be successful. If the general education teacher says the class will be studying algebraic formulas on a given day, you'll know whether your students can handle the lesson or whether they will need modifications.

Talk with the general education teacher about the kind of accommodations or modifications he or she already uses in the classroom to meet the diverse learning styles of the students. For example, a primary teacher may give pencil grips to children whose handwriting is not as well developed. And if students don't understand instructions the first time, teachers will automatically repeat, rephrase, and ask students to restate the instructions. A lot of teachers use visual organizers in their rooms—for example, writing the day's homework in a specific spot on the blackboard for students who are disorganized. Of course, this happens to be a great help for students with significant language or learning problems. Some California educators have been teaching bilingual students with strategies and methodologies that are identical to those special education teachers have been using for years.

How can special education and general education teachers get the support we need to actually implement the IEP process?

All members of the IEP team are important and have specific responsibilities. But the person representing the school system is key to actually carrying out the process. It's important that he or she has the authority to commit school or district resources and to ensure that whatever services are written into the IEP will actually be provided. It's also useful to put someone in charge of coordinating and monitoring all the services the student receives. The district is responsible for the following supports:

Time. As in dealing with any student, the school administration or district is responsible for ensuring that teachers and related service personnel have the time they need to meet, share curriculum goals and standards, and determine appropriate instructional strategies. Also, adequate planning time is an issue that can be addressed through the IEP and/or the collective bargaining process.

Personnel support. IDEA '97 allows the need for "supplementary aids and services, program modifications, or support for school personnel" to be written into the student's IEP. Once in an IEP, these must be honored by the school system because the IEP is a legally binding document.

Staff development. General education teachers may need appropriate training to fully participate and understand their role in the IEP process. Special education personnel may need specific training to help them become more knowledgeable about the general curriculum, state standards, and benchmarks. Some states are including mandatory special education instruction for teacher candidates and veteran teachers. And many states require ongoing professional development for practicing teachers in order to maintain their licenses.

Collaboration skills. The IEP team is comprised of a number of people who must work together over a period a time to best meet the needs of the student. Specific instruction in team decision making and collaboration skills can help team members write and implement an effective IEP.

IDEA SAYS

The new IDEA emphasizes the student's participation in the general curriculum and expands the IEP team to include general education teachers.

- The IEP must provide an explanation of the extent, if any, to which the student will not participate with nondisabled children in the general classroom.

- At least one of the student's general education teachers must be involved in the development of the IEP. However, the general education teacher does not have to remain in attendance throughout an entire meeting or discuss issues for which he or she has no responsibility.

- The IEP must specify the student's present levels of educational performance, how the student's disability affects progress in the general curriculum, special education and related services, supplementary aids and support services, program modifications for the student, and supports for school personnel.

- When developing a student's IEP, the IEP team must plan appropriately for what the law calls special factors, such as behavioral issues and the student's specific communication needs (blindness or visual impairment, deafness or hearing problems, or limited English proficiency). The team must also consider whether the student requires assistive technology devices and services.

- The IEP team must review a student's IEP periodically, but not less than annually, and more often if the parents or school ask for a review.

- At least every three years, the IEP team must review existing data and conduct appropriate assessments to determine if continued services are necessary.

- IEPs must include a statement of transition planning for students starting at age 14 or younger, if determined appropriate by the IEP team. Transition planning focuses on the courses of study the student needs to reach his or her post-school goals. Beginning at least by age 16, transition services help the student move from school to adult life, which can involve higher education, job training, or employment.

Myth:

The IEP can only include supports for the student, not supports for personnel who work with the student.

Reality:

Supports for school personnel to assist the student can now be written into the IEP.

Managing Paperwork

"I can teach or I can do paperwork.
Which do you want?"

Scene 1—Are You Doing Unnecessary Work?

As a speech and language pathologist, I have at least 85 IEPs a year. Between initial placements, annual reviews, dismissals, three-year evaluations, and transition IEPs, much of my paperwork has to be done at home. Are all of these forms necessary? How many hours of my own time am I expected to spend on school-related paperwork without any compensation?

A significant number of teachers are doing unnecessary paperwork because of some common misconceptions about their responsibilities under IDEA '97. Are any of the following true for you?

> **Advance planning.** Many teachers believe, or have been told by their administrators, that they cannot discuss or do paperwork for an IEP ahead of an IEP meeting. Not true! Teachers can meet to discuss and even devise a draft IEP, as long as they don't make final decisions. Teachers can also share a draft IEP with the student's parents, as long as they present it as an option. Giving parents the opportunity to review and respond to this information before the meeting can save a tremendous amount of time. In some districts, teachers are actually required to meet ahead of time with the parents. As a result, during the actual IEP meeting, teachers and parents have an opportunity to focus on the substance of the student's program, rather than the details of the IEP form.

> **Writing goals.** Some teachers believe they have to write a goal for every single class the student is taking. Also not true! You only have to write

goals for need areas. If a student's difficulties are only in reading, you don't need to write math goals. Or if a student has behavioral problems, it may not be necessary to write academic goals and objectives. Also, the entire curriculum does not need to be reflected in the goals you end up writing. All you need to do is touch on the major benchmarks.

Retesting students. Teachers may be unaware that even though reevaluation is required every three years, retesting may not be necessary. An IEP team, or other qualified persons, may review existing data—including evaluations, information provided by parents, classroom-based assessments, and the observations of teachers and related service providers—before determining whether any additional data is needed.

IEP meetings. Does your school hold too many IEP meetings? The minimum required for a student is one a year. You don't need to hold an IEP meeting unless you're changing the student's placement, the program goals, or the services that are provided—or unless the school district or parents request a meeting. An IEP that is written in the spring for an entire school year would still be active at the beginning of the next school year. It's not necessary to hold meetings at the end or beginning of each school year to revise or update an IEP that's already in effect.

Transition planning and services. The services a student will need to transition into adulthood must be addressed in an IEP when a student reaches a certain age. But it's not necessary to prepare a separate transition document.

Behavioral Intervention Plans. Some teachers are under the impression that every IEP requires a behavioral component. This is true only if the student's behavior impedes his or her learning and/or the learning of other students. The need for a Behavioral Intervention Plan may or may not be related to a student's disability.

Scene 2—Does Your State/District Require Extensive Paperwork?

My brother and I are both special education teachers. He lives in another state, and I was surprised to hear that they have half the paperwork requirements that we do. Their IEP forms average 7–10 pages, while ours average from 15–20! Why do states and local districts differ so much in the amount of paperwork they require for students with disabilities and can anything be done about it?

Several aspects of IDEA '97 were intended to reduce the amount of paperwork associated with students with disabilities. One drawback, however, is that federal law does not prevent states and individual districts from requiring additional paperwork. When the federal government first passed the original version of

IDEA in 1975, some states already had special education laws in place. The federal law was meant to be a general framework, and as long as states met the minimum requirements, specificity was left to states and local districts. In addition, some states and local districts have been tremendously impacted by litigation and education lawyers. This has led to an excess of forms, policies, and procedures designed to protect school districts from further litigation.

It's important for special education and general education teachers to know that they are equally protected under their union contracts. Everyone who teaches does paperwork at home, but if you're being asked to meet unreasonable expectations, your local affiliate should consider bargaining for release time or compensation. If you have an unusually high caseload, talk to your affiliate about bargaining for caseload and class size maximums for special education and related services personnel. If your district or state requires more paperwork than the federal government, ask your local or state affiliate to advocate for additional requirements to be dropped or minimized.

Have any affiliates successfully advocated for reduced paperwork?

Local and state affiliates around the country are advocating for reduced paperwork and greater support for their members. The Pinellas Classroom Teachers Association in Florida successfully bargained for standardized IEPs as well as release time and compensation for additional work. Association activists in Oregon have helped enact legislation to develop a standardized state IEP form. North Carolina has recently passed a "Reduction of Paperwork in Public Schools" bill that gives educators the right to refuse to provide data they've already provided elsewhere.

Teachers should be actively involved with their state and local affiliates to ensure that the work they're doing is in compliance with IDEA '97. If you teach in a state without collective bargaining, gather data, do some comparisons, then educate union leaders and the administration. If you're spending less time teaching students, and more time filling in forms, it doesn't reflect best practice.

Is anything happening at the federal level to address the burden of additional paperwork and inequities in state requirements?

There are ongoing efforts within the Department of Education to provide clarity to states about what is required. In July 2000, the Department of Education published *A Guide to the Individualized Education Program,* a brief, reader-friendly booklet that outlines the law as it relates to IEPs (see Resources). Educators can compare the IEP outlined in this guide with their local IEP. In addition, the Office of Special Education Programs will work with states in reviewing state forms to determine whether they go beyond the federal regulations. Hopefully, with greater education and increased leadership from the Department of Education, states will start to modify their requirements.

Are any states or local school districts using special techniques to streamline paperwork? Can these be duplicated in my district?

There are electronic applications available today that allow schools to streamline paperwork for IEPs and other reporting mechanisms. Some districts use software programs that provide computer-generated IEP forms. Some use an Internet-based performance management system that helps teachers write an IEP and track the workflow process for a student from referral to exit. Using a laptop, the IEP team can log on to the Internet site, type in their school district information, and get an IEP form that's tailored to an individual student and customized to their district's specifications. The system walks the team step-by-step through the entire workflow of the meeting, then generates a finished IEP in English or Spanish. If anyone on the team has a question about a specific topic, such as student eligibility, they can type in the word to immediately access what IDEA '97, their state regulations, and their district guidelines say about the topic.

IDEA SAYS

The new federal regulations have eliminated some of the old paperwork requirements:

- It's not necessary for IEPs to include goals or objectives in areas that do not affect the student's ability to progress in the general education curriculum. The purpose of IEP goals and objectives is to enable teachers and parents to gauge how well the student is progressing at intermediate times during the year. The team may use short-term objectives or benchmarks.

- Student reevaluations are still required every three years, but retesting may not be necessary. An IEP team, or other qualified persons, can review the existing data to determine whether any additional data is needed.

- Transition planning and services can be addressed within the body of the IEP. A separate document is not needed.

- IEPs only have to describe transition services that are provided for a student. They no longer have to justify transition services that are not provided.

- When a student with disabilities graduates from high school with a regular high school diploma, no reevaluation is required—only a prior written notice of the change of placement.

Myth:

All IEP forms are extensive and lengthy because of IDEA '97 paperwork requirements.

Reality:

The length of IEP forms varies across the country because states and local districts can request more paperwork than is required under federal law. The sample IEP form in the Department of Education's *Guide* is just five pages long.

4

Dealing with Discipline

"If a general education student causes a major disruption in my classroom, I can discipline him. But if my special education student causes a disturbance, I'm not allowed to do a thing! Is this fair?"

Scene 1—Aggressive Behavior in the Classroom

I have a child with autism in my classroom who receives special education services. Tom has hit and attacked teachers and other students on a number of occasions, but my principal refuses to discipline him in any way. We've been told that Tom can't be suspended because he's in the special education program. What can I do to protect myself and my other students from being hurt?

You definitely have some options for dealing with Tom's behavior. Under the new law, educators have greater flexibility in handling discipline issues involving students with disabilities. There are two questions you need to answer:

1. What is your schoolwide discipline policy?

2. Does Tom have a Behavioral Intervention Plan?

We do have a schoolwide discipline policy, but as far as I know, there is no special plan to deal with Tom's behavior. I was just told to stay out of his way.

A student with behavioral problems who receives special education and related services may need a positive Behavioral Intervention Plan, or BIP. The BIP is a set of positive behavioral supports, strategies, and interventions that address a student's behavior. If an IEP team even has an inkling that a student may have behavioral issues, we recommend that a Functional Behavioral Assessment is completed and a BIP is written based on that assessment. The

BIP should ideally be presented at the first IEP meeting. And, keeping in mind the student's right to confidentiality, that plan may need to be communicated to staff and other students who come into contact with the student in question.

How do I set this process in motion? Who can advise me about a behavioral plan for Tom?

Perhaps there is a some kind of behavioral plan in place and it was just never communicated to all of Tom's teachers. If there is no plan, however, you have the right to ask for any evaluation that seems appropriate. Start by talking to the special education teacher who is responsible for Tom's program or to the school psychologist or behavioral specialist in your district. They would be best qualified to outline the steps you need to take to address your concerns.

Do I have to wait a long time? How long should this process take?

It will vary from district to district, but it should only take a couple of weeks.

What can the school do about Tom's behavior while this process is taking place?

This is where the schoolwide discipline policy comes into play. The law gives school officials the authority to discipline all students in the same manner. If nondisabled students can be removed for violating the school code of conduct, school officials can remove students with disabilities for up to 10 consecutive school days. This 10-day period will give Tom's IEP team the time they need to discuss the situation and formulate a plan. If Tom is removed a second time, and if the number of days he is out of school total more than 10, the IEP team must conduct a Functional Behavioral Assessment and develop or review Tom's Behavioral Intervention Plan.

What do I do as a last resort—if our school officials are so worried about a lawsuit, they won't allow any disciplinary action?

First, contact your local or state affiliate. They should be able to help you work with your state department of education to pursue the appropriate action. Each state now has a special education division that monitors how schools are implementing the new IDEA. If you encounter roadblocks, there are other channels you can follow. You may want to contact the state department of special education or the U.S. Department of Education's Office of Civil Rights.

Scene 2—Guns and Drugs in School

A year ago, two of our students brought a shotgun to school and threatened their classmates with it. One boy was a general education student and the other was a special education student. The general education student was immediately removed from school pending an expulsion hearing and then was expelled. The special education student was suspended but was back in school in just three days! Is there anything in the new law to protect us against this type of situation?

Yes, under the current law, the site administrator can place a student with a disability who brings illegal drugs or weapons to school in an interim alternative educational placement for up to 45 days. The interim placement, under some conditions, can be home instruction.

Does our school have to provide a full-time teacher for the student?

No, as long as the student is provided with access to the general education curriculum and advances toward achieving his or her IEP goals.

What steps should our school take while the student is in interim alternative placement?

The IEP team should be meeting to:

- Review the appropriateness of the student's placement. If the student is dangerous, maybe a public high school isn't the best place to complete his or her education.

- Conduct a Manifestation Determination to determine whether the incident is related to the student's disability. For instance, if the student uses a wheelchair solely because of a physical disability, there's probably no direct link between the disability and bringing a gun to school. You can expel him or her just as you would a general education student who brought a gun to school and threatened classmates. If the student is severely emotionally disturbed, however, there probably is a disability link. You can't expel the student, but the IEP team must review the IEP to ensure that it's been properly implemented and that all essential supports have been provided. It may be necessary to make changes in the program or move the student to a more therapeutic environment.

What if we decide to remove the student from our school and place him in another environment after the 45 days are up and his parents disagree with our decision?

The parents may ask for an expedited hearing to challenge the IEP team's decision. During that time, the student would stay in the interim alternative setting pending the decision of the hearing officer. However, if your school feels that the student is dangerous, school officials can request an expedited hearing, in front of a due process hearing officer, to ask for an additional 45 days while they try to work out a solution.

The IEP team needs to be very proactive during the initial 45-day period. Don't wait until the 45th day to get a plan in place. This gives you some lead time in case the parents disagree with your decision and you have to request a hearing.

What if our school is directed by the courts to accept this student after the 45-day period?

The student's IEP team needs to develop a Behavioral Intervention Plan to address the situation. Again, it's critical for the team to be proactive during this period. If the student is returning, there are ongoing issues you will need to address. Don't just regard this period as a suspension. It's a window of time that allows you to examine options for addressing this student's behavior.

If you feel you need more support systems in place to teach this student, and you are not getting what you need from your school or district, the student's parents can be your greatest ally. If the parents understand what their child's teacher requires in order to be successful, they will advocate for what you need.

Finally, if you still feel threatened by a student's behavior, you should take the same steps you would take if you feel threatened by a student without a disability. Nothing precludes you from reporting the student's behavior to local law enforcement officials and filing a complaint—or pursuing a "Stay Away" order to prohibit the student from being in close proximity to you. And, of course, you can always contact your local affiliate to seek assistance.

IDEA SAYS

The new regulations offer educators more options in the disciplinary actions they can take with disruptive students who receive special education:

- School personnel can remove a student with a disability for up to 10 consecutive school days at a time for a violation of the school code of conduct, to the same extent applied to nondisabled students. The school can immediately remove for up to 10 consecutive days the same student for separate incidences of misconduct.

- School personnel can order a change of placement of a student to an appropriate interim alternative educational setting for up to 45 days for possession of weapons or illegal drugs—or the solicitation or sale of controlled substances while at school and school functions. The alternative placement setting is determined by the IEP team and can be home instruction or a facility run by the school district.

- If school personnel believe that a student is dangerous to herself or others, they can ask a hearing officer in an expedited due process hearing to remove the student to an interim alternative educational setting for up to 45 days.

- Interim alternative placements that last for 45 days can be extended in additional 45-day increments if the hearing officer agrees that the student continues to be substantially likely to injure himself or others if returned to his prior placement.

- School personnel can remove a student with a disability, including suspending or expelling, for behavior that is not a manifestation of the disability, to the same extent they would remove nondisabled students for the same behavior.

- School personnel can report crimes to appropriate law enforcement and judicial authorities. They also can ask a court for a temporary restraining order to protect children or adults from harmful behaviors.

Myth:

You can only remove a student with a disability from school for a maximum of 10 school days.

Reality:

The new law allows you to remove a student with a disability for more than 10 school days, but certain policies and procedures kick in if the suspension lasts for more than a 10-day period.

5

Training Teachers and Support Staff

"I've been teaching for 20 years and schools have changed so much. I haven't been trained to handle the special needs of the kids who are being placed in my classroom. I'm not even sure where to start!"

Scene 1—Getting the Training You Need

Maria, one of my new students, has Down syndrome. Among other difficulties, Maria has severe speech and hearing problems. I don't have special education certification, and I really don't know much about Down syndrome. How do I prepare for my new responsibilities?

It helps to know you're not alone. Maria's education is a team effort. Don't hesitate to ask the special education teacher, speech and language pathologist, or school psychologist for any advice or training you need to work effectively with Maria. Talk with these specialists about the kinds of modifications and accommodations you may need to use in your classroom.

Most important, Maria's IEP team should make sure that you and any other site personnel who work with Maria get the training you need to implement the goals and objectives in Maria's program.

Are you saying that training for staff can be written into a student's IEP?

Yes, IDEA '97 allows for training for education personnel to be included in the IEP under "supports for school personnel." Once supports are written into the IEP, the school district is required to make these resources available.

Does training for education personnel include support staff as well as teachers?

IDEA '97 requires that education support staff, including paraeducators, receive appropriate training. One of the major improvements under the new law is that paraeducators are now recognized as staff members who provide services to children with disabilities. Paraeducators often function as the teacher's right hand in the classroom. In many instances, paraeducators end up being primarily responsible for administering services to students with special needs, while the classroom teachers and special education teachers directly supervise and monitor the program.

Paraeducators not only assist the students with their lessons; in some states, they dispense medications and provide other physical services. As a result, paraeducators need training in administering special services, while many general and special education teachers need training in managing and supervising paraeducators. Any states that are applying for state improvement grants must address the training of paraeducators in their applications.

What kind of training should I have written into the IEP?

Several kinds of training are available to help you do your job more effectively:

General training. Educators are taught how to meet diverse learning needs—including special education—within a larger classroom environment. They learn about appropriate instructional strategies and how to make accommodations and curriculum modifications. Sometimes general training consists of "awareness" classes on the various kinds of disabilities.

Child-specific training. Educators are taught how to work with specific students or disabilities. For instance, if you are teaching a student with Down syndrome who has speech and hearing problems, you might receive instruction in sign language or a picture board communication system. This system allows nonverbal children who know enough words to hold a "conversation" by pointing to pictures or symbols on a board. Children with severe speech problems often use augmentative communication devices. These can range from the simple to the highly technological, like the computerized voice synthesizer used by Stephen Hawking, the eminent theoretical physicist.

Curriculum training. Educators are taught how to write goals and objectives that relate to the curriculum and state standards. Since IDEA '97 requires that students with disabilities have access to the general curriculum and classrooms, it's important for special educators to become more knowledgeable about the curriculum. Best practice advocates training special and general educators together—rather than separately—so they can benefit from a common knowledge base. It's essential that both special and general educators participate in local curriculum training and be included on the local committees that design curriculum and choose textbooks.

Where does most staff training take place and who are the instructors?

Most training takes place at the school site. Instructors may include school personnel with expertise on a given topic. Or outside experts (usually from the state, an agency, or an association) may visit the school to brief staff members on a student's needs or given disability. Experts can visit the school on a periodic basis throughout the year, and these visits can be written into a student's IEP. It's best practice for outside experts to visit the school site because it gives them the opportunity to see the student's environment and to train the staff to work within that environment.

It's also best practice for colleagues to have regular ongoing opportunities to share their expertise. Traditionally, special education and general education teachers have worked beside—but not with—each other. As public schools seek to accommodate an increasing range of students, however, teachers are being required to work collaboratively and to build a communal knowledge base. It's important for school administrations to provide the support and time that allow this collaboration to take place.

This all sounds good, but what if my district doesn't provide training for me, or the training that I receive is not adequate?

There are several steps you can take to get more information or training:

1. Talk to the special education people in your building.

2. Contact your local special education director, or the state office of the Council for Exceptional Children, to find out about courses, classes, or workshops held at the state level. Also, most districts have a certain amount of inservice or staff-development days. You can ask that issues related to inclusion and special education be included as an option for inservice training.

3. Contact the state department of education, which is required to provide training for individuals in your state.

4. Call your local and state affiliates to see if they provide training for their members. If they don't, be proactive. Talk with them about the need to establish training and resource programs.

5. Contact NEA's IDEA/Special Education Resource Cadre. The Cadre, established by NEA in January 2000, includes special education and general education practitioners from all over the country. Their primary role is to act as a resource to NEA members in the area of special education. Members of the Cadre are available to give workshops and provide training to local districts and states (see Resources).

Scene 2—Providing School Health Care Services

I'm a middle school teacher and a child with a tracheotomy is being transferred to my classroom. The principal is telling me that I'm responsible for suctioning Juan's tracheotomy tube during class. Do I really have to do this? I'm afraid of hurting him if I do something wrong.

The answer to your question really depends on what your state laws and regulations and your district's collective bargaining agreement say about who—other than a health care professional—may perform health care procedures in a school setting. In most states, the Nurse Practice Act identifies the school nurse, by virtue of his or her professional training and licensure, as the individual who determines whether or not a health care procedure may be delegated to a teacher or paraeducator. The school administrator may then actually assign the task.

Providing health care services in a school setting is a controversial and complex issue. More and more teachers and paraeducators are being called upon to provide hands-on help for medically fragile students—from feeding and diapering students to suctioning tracheotomy tubes. Under IDEA and a number of United States Supreme Court decisions, students with disabilities must receive the school health care services necessary for them to benefit from special education. The only exceptions are medical services, which are defined as those services that can only be provided by a physician or a licensed health care professional.

One of the key elements that IDEA addresses is that personnel who perform health care services must be trained and supervised by health care professionals. Training requirements differ from state to state. It's best practice for the IEP team to be aware of any health care services a student might need and, if possible, to include discussion at an IEP meeting about how these services will be conducted and by whom. Depending on the nature of the health care services, and their effect on the child's ability to benefit from his or her education, training for these services may or may not be written into the IEP. When health care services are detailed in an IEP, the team may want to obtain written instructions from the child's physician.

Do I have to perform a health care service for a student even if I feel it's not safe or the best use of my time?

This is a gray area. It may depend on what services the teacher or paraeducator is being asked to provide and the reason for refusal. Anyone who provides health care services has an obligation to the student to do so in a safe and proper manner. But some school employees may risk being charged with insubordination if they flatly refuse to perform a health care service that has been delegated by the school nurse and assigned by the administrator. It's important for school personnel to document the requests they make for additional training and supervision and seek guidance from their local and state associations if they feel they are being asked to perform procedures that may be unsafe.

Frequently, administrators who are accustomed to assigning work don't realize that school health care services are distinct from "other duties as assigned" in the job descriptions of school personnel. Teachers and paraeducators need to be advocates for themselves and their students. Is what you're being asked to do in the best interests of the student in question or the other children in your classroom?

What if something goes wrong while I'm administering health care services to a student?

Asserting the need for appropriate training and supervision is the best way to avoid problems. You should also check to see if your school district carries liability insurance that covers school personnel. In the event that something goes wrong, school personnel should immediately seek assistance from their local and state associations.

Do I have to comply if one of my students has a "do not resuscitate order"? I don't think I could just stand there and do nothing.

Medical advances now make it possible for severely ill students to attend school, but many of these students are in danger of going into cardiac or respiratory arrest while in the classroom. In a number of cases, the parents and physicians of medically fragile students have decided that certain emergency procedures, in addition to being invasive and painful, might actually worsen the students' physical problems. As a result, their physicians have issued "do not resuscitate" (DNR) orders, which causes a dilemma for many school employees.

This is an emotionally wrenching issue, which is why it's so important to gather all the facts before you're confronted with this difficult situation. Does your district require school employees to comply with DNR orders? Since this is a developing area of the law, you should consult with counsel at the state level to determine whether any special state laws or policies address this topic. While many districts honor requests to follow DNR orders, others have refused.

IDEA SAYS

IDEA '97 requires states to meet certain personnel standards in order to qualify for federal monies:

- Paraeducators are now recognized as staff members who are providing services to students with disabilities, and they must be appropriately trained and supervised in accordance with state law.
- State improvement grants must contain specific strategies for professional development and improvement for all school personnel who work with students with disabilities.
- IDEA '97 makes funding available for new technical assistance programs that provide local school districts with assistance, research, and best practices information in the area of special education.

Myth:

Educators are expected to provide specific services to children with disabilities even if they have not been trained to do so.

Reality:

IDEA '97 requires that education support staff, including paraeducators, receive appropriate training and allows for that training to be written into the IEP.

Communicating with Parents

"Some parents want services I may not have the authority or resources to deliver. I want the same thing they want for their kids—a quality education. I just can't do it alone."

Scene 1—Hands-On Parents

David's parents want constant updates on their son's progress. They're asking for daily reports, weekly lesson plans, supplemental weekend materials, and end-of-month progress reports. I'd rather have parents who are involved with their child's education than parents who are apathetic, but with 27 other children in my classroom, 8 of them with special needs, I just don't have the time for this kind of around-the-clock correspondence. Am I required to do this? What should be my response to these parents?

First you need to check on which reporting mechanisms were agreed upon in David's IEP. If the IEP includes all of the communication avenues listed above, they must be provided. However, you may be able to supply this information in ways that simplify the process and make it less burdensome for you. Also, has a provision been included in the IEP giving you the time or staff support you need to meet these parents' expectations? If not, you may want to advocate for additional support. (See Chapter 2, "Developing IEPs" and Chapter 3, "Managing Paperwork.")

If the reporting mechanisms David's parents are requesting are not listed in the IEP, you are under no obligation to provide all of them. In either case, talk with David's parents about their expectations. Are the reports they're requesting germane to IEP goals? Ask whether they would be satisfied with a modified version of their requests. Offer a number of communication options:

Phone calls & E-mail. Is it possible to send a quick E-mail or make a brief phone call rather than writing a daily report?

Check-off sheets. Can you send a customized check-off sheet home daily or weekly for different lessons or tasks the student has competed? In the IEP meeting, establish the work or behaviors you'll be monitoring. Then set up a simple checksheet to record the student's progress. For instance, the categories for one student's checksheet might include on-task behaviors, task completion, social interaction, and class discussion.

Annotated lesson plans. Can an annotated weekly lesson plan take the place of an extra report? You can make brief annotations indicating the modifications you're making for a particular student. For instance, the class will complete 20 math problems each day, but the student in question will complete 10.

Hotlines and Web sites. Does the school have a hotline parents can call or a Web site they can visit to check on homework assignments for a particular class?

Weekend homework. Rather than creating extra assignments for the weekend, you can send home classwork or homework the student didn't complete during the week. Having a chance to finish the work they've begun in class helps reinforce the lesson and helps students better understand the concepts they've been studying.

Progress reports. The law requires teachers to report progress towards annual goals at least as often for students with disabilities as they do for nondisabled students. Progress reports can include standard parent-teacher conferences, interim reports, and comments written on school report cards.

If David's parents are inflexible or unwilling to compromise and you continue to feel you have an unreasonable workload, discuss the situation with your administrator. He or she may be able to intervene on your behalf and explain to the parents why their expectations may be excessive. Point out that an excess of paperwork and record keeping can interfere with actual teaching time. Stress to parents that you all have the same priority—to provide their child with a good education.

If you are unable to come to an understanding with David's parents, you may want to contact your local affiliate. There may be language in your contract agreement that would allow you to grieve the expectations of an unreasonable workload.

Scene 2—Hard-to-Reach Parents

I teach a student with behavioral difficulties who is refusing to do her work. Even though I've made repeated attempts to contact Amy's mother, she won't come in for a conference and seldom returns my phone calls. She also has not responded to the school's request to set up another IEP meeting for Amy. Can we hold an IEP meeting if Amy's mother is not in attendance?

IDEA '97 says that an IEP meeting may be conducted without parents if the school has made a good faith effort to convince the parents to attend. However, the school should keep a record of its attempts to arrange a mutually agreed upon time and place of meeting—such as logs of phone calls, copies of letters and E-mails, and records of visits to the parents' home or workplace.

Your school must take all of the necessary steps to ensure that Amy's mother can participate fully in the IEP meeting: notifying her early enough to make sure she has an opportunity to attend, scheduling the meeting for a time when she is able to make it, providing her with all the information regarding the meeting and her rights as a parent, and arranging for an interpreter, if necessary. If Amy's mother is unable to be physically present at the IEP meeting, she may participate by phone.

If Amy's mother does not attend the meeting, can the IEP team make decisions without her input? Can she later challenge the decision and refuse permission for something that has been written into Amy's IEP?

The team can make decisions about Amy's IEP, especially if her goals and objectives remain essentially the same as those her mother agreed to previously. However, under IDEA, Amy's mother has the right to challenge any decisions about eligibility, evaluation, placement, or services her child will receive.

If parents don't agree to their child's IEP program within a certain time period, the school may choose to initiate due process procedures to induce the parents to make a decision regarding special education services.

Scene 3—Parents as Advocates

I've always loved teaching, but I'm so overwhelmed this year, I have to keep reminding myself why I originally chose this profession. My classroom is overcrowded, I don't have any assistance, and several students with both physical and learning disabilities have been placed in my classroom. I want to make sure these students get all the support they need, but I feel powerless. What can I do?

The parents of students who receive special education can be your strongest advocates for the supports you need to teach their children. When talking to parents, it's critical to communicate exactly what you need in the way of materials, time, or staff. Since parents are not answerable to school administrators, they can step forward and ask for needed supports even when teachers feel powerless to advocate for themselves. Needless to say, communication with parents regarding needed supports that you may not be getting should be diplomatic and professional.

The law allows teachers and parents to meet and discuss information concerning a child's IEP before the IEP meeting takes place, as long as no final decisions are made. Teachers are even allowed to share a draft IEP with the student's parents, provided they present it as an option. This exchange of information helps to build a sense of trust and shared goals and helps the team avoid surprises and frustration at the actual IEP meeting.

Parents are key members of the IEP team. They must be properly notified and given the opportunity to be involved in the decision making for their child. They have input into the entire process—what kind of evaluations will be conducted, what their child's goals and objectives will be, and what kind of special education and related services their child will receive. Even though the team makes decisions as a group, they need the parents' permission to implement those decisions. That's why it's especially critical for the team to understand what the parents' goals are for their child and to work toward those goals.

What if the parents' goals for their child are unrealistic?

IDEA '97 requires the IEP to consider the strengths of the child and the concerns of the parents. In fact, the language in the IEP should reference any concerns the parents may have. Most teachers have found, however, that by working with the child's parents, they can usually move them toward a more realistic understanding of their child's level of performance.

When teachers are able to communicate to parents that they share the same central goal—to provide a good education for students in an environment that nurtures and challenges them—they win powerful educational allies.

IDEA SAYS

IDEA '97 has given parents of children with disabilities a more active voice in the education of their children:

- Before the school can provide a student with special education and related services for the first time, the child's parents must give their written permission.

- The school must take steps to ensure that one or both parents of a student with a disability are present at each IEP meeting or are given the opportunity to participate. This includes notifying parents of the meeting early enough to enable them to attend, scheduling the meeting at a mutually agreed-upon time and place, and providing them with all the necessary information regarding the meeting and their rights as parents.

- The school must take whatever actions are necessary to ensure that parents understand the proceedings at an IEP meeting, including arranging for an interpreter for parents with deafness or parents whose native language is not English.

- The school must provide parents with a copy of their child's IEP at no cost to the parents.

- Parents have input into the entire IEP decision-making process—including what kind of evaluations will be conducted, what their child's goals and objectives will be, and what kind of special education and related services their child will receive.

- An IEP meeting may be conducted without the parents if the school is unable to convince the parents to attend. However, the school should keep detailed records of its attempts to contact the parents, including logs of phone calls, copies of correspondence, and records of visits made to the parents' home or workplace.

Myth:

Teachers cannot meet with parents to discuss goals and objectives for a student prior to the IEP meeting.

Reality:

As long as no final decisions are made, IDEA allows teachers and parents to meet and discuss information concerning a child's IEP before the IEP meeting takes place.

Resources

NEA RESOURCES

Print

National Education Association. 2000. *The NEA Paraeducator Handbook.*
Washington, D.C.
This handbook provides information about training and professional development as required by IDEA '97. Paraeducators, local education associations and unions, state governments, and local school districts will find a framework for establishing, developing, and maintaining a comprehensive professional development program.

————. n.d. *NEA Report on the Individuals with Disabilities Education Act (IDEA).*
Washington, D.C.
This brochure summarizes the key points of IDEA '97 in the areas that most affect NEA members, namely, how discipline, the IEP, paperwork reduction, training and professional development for school personnel, mediation, funding issues, and other services are handled at the local level.

————. 2000. *Paraeducators and IDEA: What Paraeducators Need To Know To Advocate for Themselves.* Washington, D.C.
Under the Individuals with Disabilities Education Act 1997 (IDEA '97), every state must develop laws, regulations, or written policies for the appropriate training and supervision of paraeducators who work with students with disabilities. IDEA '97, however, does not provide specifications for that training and supervision. This brochure is designed to provide paraeducators with the skills and approaches they need to be their own advocates. It also provides information for inservice and other training programs for paraeducators, the teachers they work with, and others on the educational team.

————. n.d. *Summary of the NEA Study on the Individuals with Disabilities Education Act (IDEA).* Washington, D.C.
This summary provides an understandable analysis of those sections of IDEA '97 that have the most dramatic impact on NEA members' work lives.

Video

National Education Association. 2000. *Paraeducators and the IDEA.* Washington, D.C.: Author.
This video is intended to be used in training and professional development settings in conjunction with *Paraeducators and IDEA: What Paraeducators Need To Know To Advocate for Themselves* and *The NEA Paraeducator Handbook.*

NEA IDEA/Special Education Resource Cadre

The NEA/IDEA Special Education Resource Cadre, appointed by NEA President Bob Chase in February 2000, assists NEA members nationwide with obtaining information about IDEA '97 and with its implementation. Resource Cadre members have received intensive training on IDEA issues and are available to deliver presentations on this topic. Many work with the Associations of Service Providers Implementing IDEA Reforms in Education (ASPIIRE) to develop products and information that will be used for professional development.

Cadre Members (by region)

Regional Office	Cadre Members
Northeast 220 Forbes Road, Suite 100 Braintree, Massachusetts 02184 (781) 848-0820	Judith Basa, New Jersey Ron Benner, Connecticut Patti Ralabate, Connecticut
Mid-Atlantic 1201 16th Street, NW, Suite 412 Washington, D.C. 20036 (202) 822-7111	Mary Binegar, Ohio Charlene L. Christopher, Virginia Rosemary King Johnston, Maryland M. Elaine Kresge, Kentucky
Southeast 1745 Phoenix Boulevard, Suite 330 Atlanta, Georgia 30349 (770) 996-9047	Walker McGinnis, Alabama Charles Nelson, Arkansas Barbara Taub-Albert, Florida Sarah Thomas, Mississippi
Midwest Alamo Plaza 1401 17th Street, Suite 950 Denver, Colorado 80202 (303) 293-8772	Ellen Dunn, North Dakota Cheryl Ervin, Michigan Sharon Schultz, Indiana
West Alamo Plaza 1401 17th Street, Suite 950 Denver, Colorado 80202 (303) 293-8772	Bernadette Ortega, New Mexico Katherine Starrett, Oklahoma Carol Walsh, Colorado
Pacific 1350 Bayshore Highway, Suite 730 Burlingame, California 94010 (650) 347-6000	Ed Amundson, California Carol Comparsi, California Julie Moore, Washington Judith Richards, Oregon Noel Richardson, Hawaii

FEDERAL RESOURCES

Print

Individuals with Disabilities Education Act Amendments of 1997. U.S. Public Law 105-17. 105th Cong., June 4, 1997.

Küpper, Lisa., ed. July 2000. *A Guide to the Individualized Education Program.* Available online at http://www.ed.gov/offices/OSERS/OSEP/IEP_Guide/. This guide was developed to assist educators, parents, and state and local education agencies in implementing the requirements of Part B of the Individuals with Disabilities Education Act (IDEA), regarding Individualized Education Programs (IEPs) for children with disabilities.

Office of Special Education and Rehabilitative Services, U.S. Department of Education. March 12, 1999. Assistance to States for the Education of Children with Disabilities and the Early Intervention Program for Infants and Toddlers With Disabilities: Final Regulations, 34 CFR Parts 300 and 303. *Federal Register,* 64 (48). Washington, D.C.: Government Printing Office. For further information, call (202) 205-5507. Individuals who use a telecommunications device for the deaf (TDD) may call (202) 205-5465. Individuals with disabilities may obtain this document in an alternate format (e.g., Braille, large print, audiotape, or computer diskette) on request to the Alternate Formats Center at (202) 205-8113.

National Offices

U.S. Department of Education
Office of Special Education Programs (OSEP)
Office of Special Education and Rehabilitative Services (OSERS)
U.S. Department of Education (USDOE)
Mary E. Switzer Building
330 C Street, SW
Washington, DC 20202
(202) 205-5507 (phone/TTY)
http://www.ed.gov/offices/OSERS/OSEP/

National Information Center for Children and Youth with Disabilities (NICHCY)
Academy for Educational Development
P.O. Box 1492
Washington, DC 20013-1492
(800) 695-0285; (202) 884-8200 (phone/TTY)
(202) 884-8441 (fax)
nichcy@aed.org
http://nichcy.org

Regional Centers

Northeast Regional Resource Center (NERRC)
Learning Innovations/WestEd
20 Winter Sport Lane
Williston, VT 05495
(802) 951-8226 (phone)
(802) 951-8222 (fax)
(802) 951-8213 (TTY)
nerrc@aol.com
nerrc@wested.org
http://www.wested.org/nerrc

Northeast Regional Resource Center (auxiliary office)
Learning Innovations/WestEd
91 Montvale Avenue
Stoneham, MA 02180-3616
(781) 481-1117 (phone)
(781) 481-1120 (fax)
thidalg@wested.com
http://www.wested.org/nerrc

Mid-South Regional Resource Center (MSRRC)
Human Development Institute
University of Kentucky
126 Mineral Industries Building
Lexington, KY 40506-0051
(859) 257-4921 (phone)
(859) 257-2903 (TTY)
(859) 257-4353 (fax)
msrrc@ihdi.uky.edu
http://www.ihdi.uky.edu/MSRRC

Southeast Regional Resource Center (SERRC)
School of Education
Auburn University Montgomery
P.O. Box 244023
Montgomery, AL 36124-4023
(334) 244-3100 (phone)
(334) 244-3101 (fax)
bbeale@edla.aum.edu
http://edla.aum.edu/serrc.html

Great Lakes Area Regional Resource Center (GLARRC)
Center for Special Needs Populations
The Ohio State University
700 Ackerman Road, Suite 440
Columbus, OH 43202-1559
(614) 447-0844 (phone)
(614) 447-8776 (TTY)
(614) 447-9043 (fax)

daniels.121@osu.edu
http://www.csnp.ohio-state.edu/glarrc.htm

Mountain Plains Regional Resource Center (MPRRC)
Utah State University
1780 North Research Parkway, Suite 112
Logan, UT 84341
(435) 752-0238 (phone)
(435) 753-9750 (TTY)
(435) 753-9750 (fax)
conna@cc.usu.edu
http://www.usu.edu/~mprrc

Western Regional Resource Center (WRRC)
1268 University of Oregon
Eugene, OR 97403-1268
(541) 346-5641 (phone)
(541) 346-0367 (TTY)
(541) 346-5639 (fax)
wrrc@oregon.uoregon.edu
http://interact.uoregon.edu/wrrc/wrrc.html

Federally Funded Technical Assistance Programs

The Federal Resource Center for Special Education (FRC) is a five-year contract between the Academy for Educational Development (AED); its partner, the National Association of State Directors of Special Education (NASDSE); and the United States Department of Education, Office of Special Education Programs (OSEP). The FRC supports a nationwide technical assistance network to respond to needs of students with disabilities, especially students from under-represented populations. Through its work with the Regional Resource Centers and the technical assistance network, the FRC provides a national perspective for establishing technical assistance activities within and across regions by identifying and synthesizing emerging issues and trends.

The Federal Resource Center for Special Education (FRC)
Academy for Educational Development (AED)
1825 Connecticut Avenue, NW
Washington, DC 20009
(202) 884-8215 (phone)
(202) 884-8200 (TTY)
(202) 884-8443 (fax)
frc@aed.org
http://www.dssc.org/frc

IDEA PARTNERSHIP RESOURCES

IDEA Partnerships

The ASPIIRE and ILIAD Partnerships projects listed below are coordinated by the Council for Exceptional Children (CEC). They involve more than 30 education and related service organizations. The partners, using their areas of expertise, provide information, ideas, and technical assistance to implement IDEA '97 requirements. The main goals of the partnerships are to: coordinate resources to promote application of IDEA '97 through effective instructional practice and collaboration; aid in implementing the requirements of IDEA '97; and provide products and training opportunities.

ASPIIRE Partners

Associations of Service Providers Implementing IDEA Reforms in Education (ASPIIRE)
Headquarters: The Council for Exceptional Children (CEC)
1920 Association Drive
Reston, VA 20191-1589
(877) CEC-IDEA (toll-free phone)
(703) 264-9480 (TTY)
(703) 264-1637 (fax)
ideapractices@cec.sped.org
http://www.ideapractices.org

American Federation of Teachers
555 New Jersey Avenue, NW
Washington, DC 20001
(202) 879-4400
http://www.aft.org/

The American Occupational Therapy Association, Inc. (AOTA)
4720 Montgomery Lane
P.O. Box 31220
Bethesda, MD 20824-1220
(301) 652-2682 (phone)
(800) 377-8555 (TDD)
(301) 652-7711 (fax)
http://www.aota.org

American Speech-Language-Hearing Association (ASHA)
10801 Rockville Pike
Rockville, MD 20852
(800) 498-2071 (phone)
(301) 897-5700 (TTY)
(301) 571-0457 (fax)
http://www.asha.org/

Association for Career and Technical Education (ACTE)
1410 King Street
Alexandria, VA 22314
(800) 826-9972 (toll-free phone)
acte@acteonline.org
http://www.acteonline.org/

Division for Early Childhood
The Council for Exceptional Children (CEC)
1920 Association Drive
Reston, VA 20191-1589
(703) 620-3660 (phone)
(888) CEC-SPED (toll-free phone)
(703) 264-9446 (TTY)

National Association of School Psychologists
4340 East West Highway, Suite 402
Bethesda, MD 20814
(301) 657-0270
center@naspweb.org
http://www.naspweb.org/

National Education Association (NEA)
1201 16th Street, NW
Washington, DC 20036-3290
(202) 822-7350
http://www.nea.org/publiced/idea/

ILIAD Partners

IDEA Local Implementation by Local Administrators (ILIAD)
Headquarters: The Council for Exceptional Children (CEC)
1920 Association Drive
Reston, VA 20191-1589
(877) CEC-IDEA (toll-free phone)
(703) 264-9480 (TTY)
(703) 264-1637 (fax)
ideapractices@cec.sped.org
http://www.ideapractices.org

FAPE Partnership

The Families and Advocates Partnership for Education (FAPE) project aims to inform families, advocates, partners, and others about IDEA '97 and about research-based, best practices for developing appropriate programs for educating children and youth.

Families and Advocates Partnership for Education (FAPE)
PACER Center
4826 Chicago Avenue South
Minneapolis, MN 55417-1098
(888) 248-0822 (toll-free phone)
(612) 827-2966 (phone)
(612) 827-7770 (TTY)
(612) 827-3065 (fax)
fape@pacer.org
http://www.fape.org

Policy Maker Partnership

The Policy Maker Partnership (PMP) for Implementing IDEA '97 helps policy makers act as informed change agents who focus on improving educational outcomes for students with disabilities.

The Policy Maker Partnership (PMP) for Implementing IDEA '97
National Association of State Directors of Special Education
1800 Diagonal Road, Suite 320
Alexandria, VA 22314-2840
(703) 519-3800 (phone)
(877) IDEA-INFO (toll-free phone)
(703) 519-7008 (TTY)
(703) 519-3808 (fax)
nasdse@nasdse.org
http://www.nasdse.org

Clearinghouses

ERIC Clearinghouse for Special and Gifted Education
ERIC/OSEP Special Project
The Council for Exceptional Children
1920 Association Drive
Reston, VA 20191-1589
(800) 328-0272 (phone/TTY)
(703) 620-2521 (fax)
ericec@cec.sped.org
http://ericec.org

ERIC Clearinghouse for Special and Gifted Education funded by:
The Council for Exceptional Children (CEC)
1920 Association Drive
Reston, VA 20191-1589
(703) 620-3660 (phone)

(888) CEC-SPED (toll-free phone)
(703) 264-9446 (TTY)

National Clearinghouse for Professions in Special Education
The Council for Exceptional Children (CEC)
1920 Association Drive
Reston, VA 20191-1589
(800) 695-0285 (toll-free phone)
(703) 264-9476 (phone)
(703) 264-9480 (TTY)
(703) 264-1637 (fax)
ncpse@cec.sped.org
http://special-ed-careers.org

Print

Bateman, Barbara D. and Mary Anne Linden. 1998. *Better IEPs: How To Develop Legally Correct and Educationally Useful Programs, Third Edition.* Reston, Va.: Council for Exceptional Children.
This handbook, written by lawyer-educators, explains IEPs and IDEA '97 from a legal perspective, citing the law and court cases throughout. It spells out the do's and don'ts of placement, funding, and procedure; describes the IEP team; gives examples of problematic IEPs; and shows how to write legally and educationally sound IEPs.

Bootel, Jaclin A. and Cynthia L. Warger. *Political Advocacy Handbook.* Reston, Va.: Council for Exceptional Children.
Designed to assist special educators and other concerned individuals, this handbook is organized as a facilitator's guide for effective political advocacy.

Council for Exceptional Children. 1999. *IEP Team Guide.* Reston, Va.: Council for Exceptional Children.
This book for IEP team members explains in clear, concise, everyday language what federal law requires and guides the team through the process of developing and revising an IEP. It highlights the importance of each team member, including the student; spells out the potential contributions of each member to the child's IEP; and gives practical advice for carrying out each person's role.

Evans, Cal. 1999. *Navigating the Dual System of Discipline: A Guide for School Site Administrators.* Reston, Va.: Council for Exceptional Children.
This book gives the information necessary to understand the background of the disciplinary components of IDEA '97, explains the actual disciplinary requirements of IDEA, and presents a practical process for compliance with these requirements. Intended as a guidance and reference tool for school administrators and special education personnel, it includes helpful, reproducible forms and checklists as well as excerpts of pertinent laws and regulations. It is organized for practical use and is easy to follow.

Pickett, Anna Lou and Kent Gerlach. 1997. *Supervising Paraeducators in School Settings.* Reston, Va.: Council for Exceptional Children.
This books provides teachers and administrators with the knowledge and skills needed to manage these valuable team members. Clear and practical, this is the

first book written about issues associated with managing and supervising paraeducators: team role clarification, professional and ethical responsibilities, and administrative issues.

Siegel, Lawrence M. 1999. *The Complete IEP Guide: How To Advocate for Your Special Education Child.* Reston, Va.: Council for Exceptional Children.
This book, written by an attorney, is for parents who advocate for their special education child. It is also for administrators and counselors who need to see the process from a lawyer's view point. It explains the basics of advocacy as well as such topics as resolving disputes, filing complaints, and getting a lawyer. IDEA '97 regulations, selected regulations of 1999, and lists of support groups and government agencies are also included.

CD-ROM

Council for Exception Children. 2000. *Discover IDEA CD 2000.* Reston, Va.: Council for Exceptional Children.
The 2000 edition of this valuable resource contains topical updates from the U.S. Department of Education on critical issues plus the Headstart Disability Regulations, resources for professional development, and more. This CD-ROM has the most user-friendly versions of the IDEA regulations and over 50 policy and practices publications that answer viewers' questions as well as leading them to invaluable resources on the Web.

Electronic Application for Establishing IEPs

IdeaPro IEP Software. 1999. Reston, Va.: Council for Exceptional Children. For more information, go to http://www.cec.sped.org/bk/catalog/compres.html.
IdeaPro IEP Software is a powerful IEP writing tool designed for either Macintosh or Windows 95/98 computers. Users receive a diskette or CD-ROM that includes a number of IDEA-supportive documents; modifiable menus; fast and friendly search capabilities for student histories, goals, and benchmarks; IDEA comments and guidance on screen, as well as documentation and technical support (via telephone or Web).

Video

Bateman, Barbara D. 1999. *Understanding IDEA 1997 and the 1999 Regulations.* Reston, Va.: Council for Exceptional Children.
This tape addresses IDEA changes in team membership, the legal process, and disciplinary procedures.

————. 1999. *Legal IEPs: A Common Sense Approach.* Reston, Va.: Council for Exceptional Children.
This tape addresses how to set the stage for IEP meetings, what is legally required in an IEP, and how best to develop educationally useful IEPs.

Council for Exceptional Children. 1998. *Focus on the IEP and Performance Assessment*. Reston, Va.: Council for Exceptional Children.
This video presents experts' views on student involvement, performance assessment, benchmarks, short-term objectives, accommodations, alternative assessments, and involving the general education teacher. Presenters include: Joe Ballard, Pat Guthrie, Jonathan C. McIntire, Margaret J. McLaughlin, Alba Ortiz, and Martha Thurlow.

Council for Exceptional Children. 1998. IDEA *Reauthorization Discipline and Creating Positive Learning Environments*. Reston, Va.: Council for Exceptional Children.
This video answers questions about IDEA requirements concerning the role of the IEP team, behavioral intervention plans, suspension and expulsion, and Interim Alternative Education Settings (IAES). It also discusses positive behavioral supports, cultural differences relating to behavior, and developing safe schools.

Hanlon, Grace M. 1998. A New IDEA for Special Education: *Understanding the System and the New Law*. Reston, Va.: Council for Exceptional Children.
This video supports the importance of collaboration between parents, general educators, and special educators by introducing the requirements of IDEA '97 to parents and teachers and by highlighting the referral process, evaluation, IEPs, placement and related services, preparing for transitions, discipline, mediation, and the standardized testing requirement.

OTHER IDEA AND SPECIAL EDUCATION RESOURCES

Print

Thurlow, M.L., J.E. Elliott, and J.E. Ysseldyke. 1998. *Testing Students with Disabilities: Practical Strategies for Complying with District and State Requirements.* Thousand Oaks, Calif.: Corwin Press.

Should students with disabilities participate in district and statewide tests? How will educators make sure the requirements are met and ensure that each student's Individualized Education Program (IEP) is followed? This guide helps translate the issues surrounding state and district testing of students with disabilities into what educators need to know and do. Here are the tools to begin the process of implementing meaningful tests for all students.

Electronic Applications for Establishing IEPs

GoalView. 2000. Santa Rosa, Calif.: Learning Tools International. For more information, go to www.goalview.com.

GoalView, an Internet-based performance management system, allows schools to streamline paperwork for IEPs and other reporting mechanisms. With district goals, state standards, and more than 10,000 special education goals and objectives available in English or Spanish, teachers can write an IEP and track the workflow process for a student from referral to exit.

StudentTracker+. 1999. Moorhead, Minn.: Micro-Assessments. For more information, go to http://www.micro-assessments.com.

StudentTracker+ automates student record keeping. Institutions can customize reporting of students individually, by instructor, by classroom, by grade, or by an entire school. Instructors can manage progress notes and establish IEPs; administrators can organize and review student and faculty progress relative to written student reports. Parental and emergency information is readily accessible.

Web Sites

http://www.familyvillage.wisc.edu/index.html

Family Village is a global community that integrates information, resources, and communication opportunities on the Internet for persons with cognitive and other disabilities, for their families, and for those that provide them services and support.

http://www.nasdse.org

The National Association of State Directors of Special Education, Inc. (NASDSE) promotes and supports education programs for students with disabilities in the United States. NASDSE maintains a private library of resources, including current state special education laws and regulations, state plans, and related policy materials.

http://www.coled.umn.edu/nceo/

The National Center on Educational Outcomes provides national leadership in the participation of students with disabilities and limited English proficient students in national and state assessments, standards-setting efforts, and graduation requirements.

http://www2.edc.org/NCIP
The National Center to Improve Practice (NCIP) promotes the effective use of technology to enhance educational outcomes for students with sensory, cognitive, physical, and social/emotional disabilities.

http://www.ed.gov/offices/OSERS/NIDRR/
The U.S. Department of Education's Office of Special Education and Rehabilitative Services (OSERS), through its National Institute on Disability and Rehabilitation Research (NIDRR), conducts comprehensive and coordinated programs of research and related activities to maximize the full inclusion, social integration, employment, and independent living of disabled individuals of all ages.

http://www.schoolnet.ca/sne/
The Special Needs Education (SNE) project is an Internet service that provides resources for parents, teachers, schools, and other professionals, individuals, groups, and organizations involved in the education of students with special needs. SNE operates under the auspices of SchoolNet, a cooperative initiative of Canada's provincial, territorial, and federal governments in consultation with educators, universities, colleges, and industry.

http://TheArc.org/misc/dislnkin.html
This Web site features a detailed listing of disability-related resources that are found on the Internet.

Clearinghouses

HEATH Resource Center
American Council on Education
One Dupont Circle, NW, Suite 800
Washington, DC 20036-1193
(800) 544-3284 (phone/TTY)
(202) 833-5696 (fax)
Heath@ace.nche.edu
http://www.heath-resource-center.org

National Information Clearinghouse on Children who are Deaf-Blind (DB-LINK)
Western Oregon University
Teaching Research Division
345 North Monmouth Avenue
Monmouth, OR 97361
(800) 438-9376 (phone)
(800) 854-7013 (TTY)
(503) 838-8150 (fax)
dblink@tr.wou.edu
http://www.tr.wou.edu/dblink

Organizations Concerned with Deaf/Blind Issues

National Technical Assistance Consortium for Children and Young Adults Who Are Deaf/Blind (NTAC)
ntac@wou.edu
http:/www.tr.wou.edu/ntac

Western Oregon University
345 North Monmouth Avenue
Monmouth, OR 97361
(503) 838-8096 (phone)
(503) 838-8821 (TTY)
(503) 838-8150 (fax)

Helen Keller National Center
111 Middle Neck Road
Sands Point, NY 11050
(516) 944-8900 (phone)
(516) 944-8637 (TTY)
(516) 944-7302 (fax)
http://www.helenkeller.org/national

Organizations Concerned with Deaf–Postsecondary Issues

Midwest Center for Postsecondary Outreach (MCPO)
St. Paul Technical College
235 Marshall
St. Paul, MN 55102
(651) 221-1337 (phone/TTY)
(651) 221-1339 (fax)
rolson@stp.tec.mn.us
http://www.mcpo.org

Northeast Technical Assistance Center (NETAC)
Rochester Institute of Technology
52 Lomb Memorial Drive
Rochester, NY 14623
(716) 475-6433 (phone/TTY)
(716) 475-7660 (fax)
netac@rit.edu
http://www.netac.rit.edu

Postsecondary Education Consortium (PEC)
The University of Tennessee
2229 Dunford Hall
Knoxville, TN 37996-4020
(865) 974-0607 (phone/TTY)
(865) 974-3522 (fax)
pec@utk.edu
http://sunsite.utk.edu/cod/pec

Western Regional Outreach Center & Consortia (WROCC)
National Center on Deafness
California State University, Northridge
18111 Nordhoff Street
Northridge, CA 91330-8267
(888) 684-4695; (818) 677-2611 (phone/TTY)
(818) 677-4899 (fax)
wrocc@csun.edu
http://wrocc.csun.edu

Organizations Concerned with Early Childhood Issues

National Early Childhood Technical Assistance System (NECTAS)
Bank of America Plaza
137 East Franklin Street, Suite 500
Chapel Hill, NC 27514-3628
(919) 962-2001 (phone)
(877) 574-3194 (TTY)
(919) 966-7463 (fax)
nectas@unc.edu
http://www.nectas.unc.edu

Organizations Concerned with Finance Issues

Center for Special Education Finance (CSEF)
American Institutes for Research
1791 Arastradero Road
P.O. Box 1113
Palo Alto, CA 94302
(650) 843-8136 (phone)
(650) 493-2209 (TTY)
(650) 858-0958 (fax)
csef@air.org
http://csef.air.org

Organizations Concerned with Minority Issues

Alliance Project (Headquarters)
Peabody College, Box 160
Vanderbilt University
Nashville, TN 37203
(800) 831-6134; (615) 343-5610 (phone)
(615) 343-5611 (fax)
alliance@vanderbilt.edu
http://www.alliance2k.org/headquarters/west.htm

Alliance Project (DC Metro Office)
10860 Hampton Road
Fairfax Station, VA 22039-2700
(703) 239-1557 (phone)

(703) 503-8627 (fax)
judysd@edu.gte.net
http://www.alliance2k.org/metro/east.htm

Center for Minority Research in Special Education (COMRISE)
The University of Virginia
Curry School of Education
405 Emmet Street
Charlottesville, VA 22903-2495
(804) 924-1022 (phone)
(804) 982-HEAR (TTY)
(804) 924-0747 (fax)
tfg7y@virginia.edu
http://curry.edschool.virginia.edu/go/comrise

Organizations Concerned with Outcomes

National Center on Educational Outcomes (NCEO)
University of Minnesota
350 Elliott Hall
75 East River Road
Minneapolis, MN 55455
(612) 626-1530 (phone)
(612) 624-0879 (fax)
scott027@tc.umn.edu
http://www.coled.umn.edu/NCEO

Organizations Concerned with Parents

Parents Engaged in Education Reform (PEER)
Federation for Children with Special Needs
1135 Tremont Street, Suite 420
Boston, MA 02120
(617) 236-7210 (phone)
(617) 572-2094 (fax)
fcsninfo@fcsn.org
http://www.fcsn.org/peer

Technical Assistance Alliance for Parent Centers—the Alliance
PACER Center
4826 Chicago Avenue South
Minneapolis, MN 55417-1098
(888) 248-0822; (612) 827-2966 (phone)
(612) 827-7770 (TTY)
(612) 827-3065 (fax)
alliance@taalliance.org
http://www.taalliance.org

Organizations Concerned with Personnel Preparation

Professional Development Leadership Academy: Enhancing Collaborative Partnerships for Systems Change
National Association of State Directors of Special Education
1800 Diagonal Road, Suite 320
Alexandria, VA 22314-2840
(703) 519-3800 (phone)
(703) 519-7008 (TTY)
(703) 519-3808 (fax)
karlm@nasdse.org
http://www.nasdse.org

Organizations Concerned with Technology Issues

LINK•US: Center To Link Urban Schools with Information and Support on Technology and Special Education
Education Development Center, Inc.
55 Chapel Street
Newton, MA 02458-1060
(617) 969-7100 (phone)
(617) 964-5448 (TTY)
(617) 969-3440 (fax)
linkus@edc.org
http://www.edc.org/LLINKUS

Organizations Concerned with Transition Issues

Academy for Educational Development
1875 Connecticut Ave., NW
Washington, DC 20009
(202) 884-8209 (phone)
(202) 884-8443 (fax)
nta@aed.org
http://www.dssc.org/nta

National Transition Network (NTN)
Institute on Community Integration
University of Minnesota
102 Pattee Hall
150 Pillsbury Drive SE
Minneapolis, MN 55455
(612) 624-1062 (phone)
(612) 624-8279 (fax)
johns006@tc.umn.edu
http://ici2.coled.umn.edu/ntn/

Other Organizations

Center on Positive Behavioral Interventions and Supports
5262 University of Oregon
Eugene, OR 97403-5262
(541) 346-2505 (phone)
(541) 346-5689 (fax)
pbis@oregon.uoregon.edu
http://www.pbis.org

Consortium for Appropriate Dispute Resolution in Special Education (CADRE)
Direction Service
P.O. Box 51360
Eugene, OR 97405-0906
(541) 686-5060 (phone)
(541) 686-5063 (fax)
cadre@directionservice.org
http://www.directionservice.org/cadre

National Center on Education, Disability, and Juvenile Justice (EDJJ)
Department of Special Education
University of Maryland
College Park, MD 20742-1161
(301) 405-6489 (phone)
(301) 314-9158 (fax)
p111@umail.umd.edu
http://www.edjj.org

Project FORUM
National Association of State Directors of Special Education
1800 Diagonal Road, Suite 320
Alexandria, VA 22314-2840
(703) 519-3800 x335 (phone)
(703) 519-7008 (TTY)
(703) 519-3808 (fax)
joy@nasdse.org
http://www.nasdse.org/forum.htm